Sarah Snell has been writing poetry since her early teens, *'Crime and Punishment'*, her first, when she was fifteen. Much of her inspiration came from schoolfriends as well as her family. She makes her home in Hull with her little green budgie, Kiwi and he has a little friend, a grey budgie, Smokey. Her past employments include working as a shop assistant at Tradex and as a counter clerk in a post office. She is currently a parcel courier.

My loving parents who helped to inspire me, and my beloved grandparents who were always there for me.

Sarah Snell

A FANTASTICAL POETRY COLLECTION

AUSTIN MACAULEY PUBLISHERS™
LONDON * CAMBRIDGE * NEW YORK * SHARJAH

Copyright © Sarah Snell 2024

The right of Sarah Snell to be identified as author of this work has been asserted by the author in accordance with sections 77 and 78 of the Copyright, Designs and Patents Act 1988.

All rights reserved. No part of this publication may be reproduced, stored in a retrieval system, or transmitted in any form or by any means, electronic, mechanical, photocopying, recording, or otherwise, without the prior permission of the publishers.

Any person who commits any unauthorised act in relation to this publication may be liable to criminal prosecution and civil claims for damages.

A CIP catalogue record for this title is available from the British Library.

ISBN 9781398498662 (Paperback)
ISBN 9781398498679 (ePub e-book)

www.austinmacauley.com

First Published 2024
Austin Macauley Publishers Ltd®
1 Canada Square
Canary Wharf
London
E14 5AA

Austin Macauley Publishers for making this possible.

Table of Contents

If You	**17**
If I Were	**18**
In the Land Of	**19**
The Message	**20**
Fantasy	**21**
What Is Poetry?	**22**
Christmas Memories	**23**
Robin	**24**
My Dream	**25**
Christmas Is Near	**26**
Christmas Time	**27**
Shine	**28**
Christmas Song	**29**
The Park	**30**
Holiday	**31**
The Journey	**32**

My Life	**34**
Love Is Not Simple	**35**
Spring	**36**
Summer	**37**
Autumn	**38**
Winter	**39**
Daytime	**40**
People	**41**
What Are You Like?	**42**
Crime and Punishment	**43**
Thunder	**45**
Emotions	**46**
Opposites Attract	**47**
Night-Time	**48**
The Crow	**49**
Some Similes	**50**
Numbers	**51**
A Grand Adventure	**52**
What About Me?	**53**
The Sweet Boy	**54**
Freedom	**55**
A Birthday Run	**56**
Colours	**57**

The Bird	**58**
Seasons	**59**
What to Eat?	**60**
What a Sight	**61**
The Storm	**62**
A Precious Thing	**63**
Whales and Dolphins	**64**
Butterfly	**65**
Bingo	**66**
The Little Crab	**67**
Darts	**68**
What Is a Baby?	**69**
Sunrise	**71**
The Country Road	**72**
More Similes	**73**
Weather Patterns	**74**
The Grand Day Out	**75**
My Puppy	**76**
Bunch of Gibberish	**77**
Retirement	**78**
At the Airport	**79**
Train Ride	**80**
Wind, Sun and Snow	**81**

My Story	82
I Can Dance	83
The Colours of Life	84
Final Words	85
Vampires	86
Me, A Vampire	87
Slayer	88
My Last Night	89
Vampire Tale	90
The Stranger	91
Vampire Mini Poems	92
Witches	93
All About Witches	94
Tale of the Witches	95
What Are Witches?	96
What a Sight!	97
My Friend, the Witch	98
Witch Mini Poems	99
Werewolves	100
The Transformation	101
Werewolf Haikus	102
The Werewolf	103
What Is a Werewolf?	104

Full Moon	**105**
The Wolf	**106**
Werewolf Mini Poems	**107**
Ghosts	**108**
Anyone There?	**109**
A Ghost's Song	**110**
Poltergeist	**111**
Haunted House	**112**
What Does a Ghost Look Like?	**113**
The Plight	**114**
The Ghost	**115**
Noises in an Empty House	**116**
Ghost Mini Poems	**117**
Dragons	**118**
To Know a Dragon	**119**
What Are Dragons Like?	**120**
Many Dragons	**121**
Take Flight	**122**
A Proud Dragon	**123**
What Can a Dragon Do?	**124**
Dragon Mini Poems	**125**
Mythical Beings	**126**
Fairies	**127**

The Fairy	128
The Elegance of Unicorns	129
Unicorns	130
Demons	131
What Is a Demon?	132
Demons, What Are They Like?	133
The Mermaid	134
Mermaids	135
Nymphs	136
Elf	137
Imaginary Friend (Part 1)	138
Imaginary Friend (Part 2)	139
Leprechaun	140
Lost	141
Hades	142
Father Christmas	143
Christmas Time	144
Be Good at Christmas	145
Angels	146
What Is an Angel?	147
Supernatural	148
How to Recognise a Supernatural Being?	149
A World of Fantasy	150

Supernatural Beings	**151**
Miscellaneous Mini Poems 1	**152**
Miscellaneous Mini Poems 2	**153**

If You

If you stay true
You'll never be blue

If you are mean
You'll never be seen

If you are nice
You'll never be spice

If you smell great
You'll never wait

If you are bold
You'll never be cold

If you are kind
We'll keep you in mind.

If I Were

A mammal, what would I be?
I would be a lion
So that I'd be free

A sea creature, what would I be?
I would be a dolphin
Living in the sea

A bird, what would I be?
I would be a seagull
Flying to a quay

On holiday, where would I go?
I would go north
To see the Aurora light show

Anything in the world, what would I be?
Are you kidding?
I'd rather be me.

In the Land Of

In the land of the horse
What do you see?
A horse running wild
Is a horse running free

In the world of the dog
What do you know?
A dog that is healthy
Is a dog on the go

In the world of the cat
What will you find?
A cat that is happy
Is a cat that is kind

In the land of the living
What will you learn?
All creatures are the same
Of information, they yearn.

The Message

A message will come
From high up above
It's a message of peace
It's a message of love

And in that message
The one from above
That message of peace
Has drawn in it, a dove

A dove is a symbol
A symbol well known
Of peace and prosperity
In the place you call home

In home is your love
It lies in your heart
With it comes great peace
Even that is a start.

Fantasy

In fantasy I find
My own piece of mind

It's how I unwind
To the ties that bind

Then I start to feel kind
After light has been shined

And when I start to wind
I finish.

What Is Poetry?

It is a song
Blowing on a gentle breeze

It is a rhythm
Beating steadily in your heart

It is a friendship
One that will never leave

It is a memory
Of joy and happiness from the start

It is love
That is felt with every breath
It is you

And knowing that we'll never part.

Christmas Memories

It's Christmas again
I remember back when

At Christmas, it glowed
With the falling snow

In these memories of mine
It has been such a long time

Since that very pretty sight
Occurred one Christmas night.

Robin

In the frost of mid-winter
When snow starts to fall
You may see a robin
Come to give you a call

Once every year
In your garden, you'll find
Your robin returns
In nature it is kind

Then many years later
Though it may be cold
One last time it comes
For now, it is old.

My Dream

Oh how I dream to be
Fluffy as a bunny
Might be kinda funny

Oh how I dream to be
Stronger than a bear
Living in his lair

Oh how I dream to be
Healthy as a horse
Running its course

Oh how I dream to be
Cuter than a kitten
Feeling rather smitten

Oh how I dream to be
Slyer than a fox
Avoiding falling rocks

Oh what a dream…

Christmas Is Near

With stars shining bright
And days mostly night
You know it's Christmas soon

We'll go to a ball
Then snow starts to fall
And it is Christmas soon

With houses well lit
More than a bit
It's Christmas coming soon

Gifts under the tree
It's easy to see
That it's Christmas soon.

Christmas Time

When Christmas time comes knocking
And all your friends are near
All you need this Christmas
Is a bit of festive cheer

And Christmas day morning
You come downstairs and see
All those wonderful presents
Underneath the Christmas tree

After opening the presents
You settle down to play
With those excellent toys
That this Christmas, came your way

Now it's after dinner
It's time to say goodnight
As everybody goes upstairs
Whisper to all, sleep tight.

Shine

Shine like a light
Like a star shining bright

Glow like the sun
Like a child having fun

Shine like the moon
Like a big white balloon

Glow like the sand
Like water slipping through the hand.

Christmas Song

Christmas comes but once a year
And all around is festive cheer

There are lots of presents beneath the tree
Lots of joy for the family

The happiest day, with faces aglow
Let us all hope and dream of snow

On the night, after the day
When all are merry, that is the way

So a day of fun and having a ball
Has come to an end
Now deck the halls.

The Park

I sit on a bench
At the centre of the park
It turns dark
As I think

I think of the children
Walking home through the park
As it turns dark
And I think

I think of the people
Walking dogs in the park
Now it is dark
And I think

What a lovely place to be
Now it is dark
In this beautiful park.

Holiday

I want to go on holiday
Where can I go?
I might go to Alaska
Where there will be snow

I want to go on holiday
Where should it be?
I could go to Spain
So close to the sea

I want to go on holiday
Where can I try?
I'd like to try Australia
But I would need to fly

I want to go on holiday
Where can I choose?
I'll go around the Med
On a fabulous cruise.

The Journey

As I walk through the fields in the setting sun
At a very brisk walk but hardly a run
It is oh so bright in the falling sun
It's here, it's now, the night has begun

I walk to the forest by the light of the moon
At my brisk walk, I'll be there soon
It is so lovely in the light of the moon
It's coming, ever closer, it's morning soon

Now it is morning, I haven't far to go
As I come to a house at the end of a row
The light from the sun casts a really warm glow
Over this house at the end of the row

And behind this house, a cottage standing free
Surrounded by flowers and just one tree
I see the beauty, move closer and see
A sign that says this house is for me.

There was a young man from Crewe
Who goes by the name of Drew
He'd never lie
Or hurt a fly
Because he is so honest and true

There was an old woman from Hull
Who was just a little bit dull
I got out a cane
Because she was a pain
And gave her a tap on the skull

There was a young man from Hessle
Who lives in what looks like a castle
He's kind to all
And in his hall
He teaches young kids how to wrestle

My Life

When I was two, I was so cute

When I was four, I walked to the door

When I was six, I learnt some tricks

When I was eight, I met Catherine Tate

When I was ten, I gained a friend

When I was twelve into school I delved

When I was fourteen, I joined a sports team

When I was sixteen, I met the Queen

When I was eighteen, I accomplished my dream

Now I am twenty, I think I've done plenty.

Love Is Not Simple

You may think me simple
But I assure you I am not
I can be quite sophisticated
But I love you a lot
I know how much you love me
And you're the best I've got
Please never leave my side
Since I do love you a lot

Spring

You know when spring is about to start
Because snow starts to melt
Animals start coming out again
A new season has been dealt

New greens start growing on the trees
New leaves fluttering in a spring breeze
The soft buzzing of bees fills the air
And pollen in the air makes you sneeze

These are the signs of spring arriving
A new year and feelings finally here
Smells that make you look all around
So you can see that spring is near.

Summer

It's summer time now, what can I do?
I'll go down the beach with all the family too

We'll have ice-creams
A donkey ride
And lay on the sand

It's our summer holiday, what will we do?
We'll go on a trip and perhaps try something new

We'll swim in the sea
Enjoy a lovely barbeque
And enjoy being free

Autumn

All the leaves are falling
Yellow, green and brown
A beautiful carpet of autumn leaves
Lays upon the ground

As you walk amongst them
Listen to the sound
Crunching, crackling noises
Autumn's all around

The smell in the air is fresh and clean
The animals are fast asleep
It's now goodbye to summertime
And autumn we must greet

Winter

I live in a cottage at the edge of a wood
I go for a walk along the frozen river
It makes me start to shiver

Because it's icy, it's cold, it's winter
All around the ground is pearly white
And it will stay like that through the night

The snow glistens in the wintry sun
And then, as it starts to melt
I remember the happiness I felt

By this frozen river
In winter.

Daytime

When there is daylight
You can see all around
Light shining everywhere
And people to be found

Birds singing songs
So peaceful in the trees
They carry on chirping
Through the gentle breeze

And when the sun sets
The sky turns to pink
It is so beautiful
Prettier than you think

People

Mr Magic is a man
Who can

Mrs Spell is a witch
With a twitch

Miss Sunshine is a girl
With a curl

Master Moonlight is a boy
With a toy

Lord Humble is a male
Who tells tales

Lady Luck is a singer
And a winner

All these people have one thing to share
They live in our dreams and all seem to care

What Are You Like?

You would be good
If only you could

I would be fair
If only I dared

He would be kind
If he wouldn't mind

She would be loved
If she was a dove

We could all give
To help people live

Crime and Punishment

I will tell you a story
It happened three years ago today
A story I want to forget

I committed a crime
A hideous crime
A crime I'll try to describe

There was shouting and screaming
And howling and bleeding
I didn't know what I was doing

The police found me out
And they gave a shout
But I turned and ran away

I kept racing
They kept chasing
Then they caught up to me

They stopped me
They cuffed me
They put me in their car

They took me away
I knew I would pay
For the crime that I did commit

They put me in jail
No one would pay bail
And I am still here today

Thunder

You would think the sky was falling down
When you hear the thunder roar

The lightning flashes in the sky
And then the rain starts pouring

The thunder wears a big black cloak
Which makes the earth a quiver

It even makes the mighty oak
Bend down and start to shiver

Emotions

What is love?
An emotion
A feeling of belonging
A dream

What is happiness?
It is knowledge
A lovely emotion
Of glee

What is bliss?
True love
True happiness
Being free

Opposites Attract

Opposites attract is what they say
So does that mean:-
Love likes hate?
High loves low?
Early likes late?
Fast loves slow?

Opposites attract is what they say
Does that mean:-
Deep likes shallow?
Loose loves tight?
Wide likes narrow?
Dark loves light?

Opposites attract.

Night-Time

You know it's night-time
When the sun starts to set
And the animals go to sleep

You know it's night-time
As the moon begins to rise
And the owls come out to hunt

You know it's night-time
The stars start to twinkle
And the sky becomes dark

You know it's night-time
When you begin to feel tired
Knowing it's time to go to bed.

The Crow

There's a crow sitting,
At the end of my bed
Just sitting

It's sat staring at me
From the end of my bed
Just staring

It moves occasionally from side to side
But still it sits and stares at me
From the end of my bed

It's so scary, staring at me
From the end of my bed
So scary

I want it to leave, to go,
From the end of my bed
Just leave

And never return.

Some Similes

Yellow like a flower
Round like the sun
As happy as a child
A child having fun

Blue like a bluebell
As vast as the sky
Soaring like an eagle
An eagle flying high

White like a cloud
Floating high up above
Like the wings of a bird
The wings of a dove

Red like a rose
Like love it is deep
Tired like a child
Like a child fast asleep

Numbers

One
And you're gone
Two
You are true
Three
You are free
Four
Ask for more
Five
So alive
Six
Do some tricks
Seven
You're in heaven
Eight
Don't be late
Nine
You'll be fine
Ten
Back again

A Grand Adventure

Walking through life is a journey to endure
It is an adventure which helps keep you pure

The journey is long, takes time and is hard
As if life has dealt you a really wild card

So undertake adventure, don't take it too light
Animals you encounter may start to bite

But stick to your goals, maybe you'll see
Life is not so difficult; it is as easy as can be

What About Me?

I wouldn't be me
If I didn't change my mind
Some of the time

It wouldn't be the same
If I didn't hold any blame
Now and again

I wouldn't be me
If I wasn't free
To be what I want to be

But that's just me

The Sweet Boy

I'll tell you a story
Of beauty and of joy
I will also tell you
It is about a boy

He lives down my street
And he's so very sweet
He is lovely to greet
As you walk down my street

He looks like a dream
Never making you scream
Making a good team
Like such a good dream

He'd care for anyone
Enjoys having fun
We both now must run
Now that the story is done

Freedom

If I could be free
To go where I please
I would be happy
Contented
Not sad
Or demented
Go places afar
Driving in my car
Meeting people
Seeing faces
Eating well
Going places
Then come back
Relax
Then start again.

A Birthday Run

Walking through the streets one day
A man ran up to me and said
"Hip hip hooray"
I asked
"What's that for?"
He replied
"It's my birthday today"
So I said
"You seem excited"
And he said
"I've just turned forty"
I said
"You look kind of sporty"
He replied
"To celebrate my birthdays, I run"
So I said
"For charity?"
Then he said
"No. Just for clarity"
Then he ran off.

Colours

"What's your favourite colour?"
I said to the man down the road
"My favourite colour is green," he said
"It's the colour of my toad."

"What's your favourite colour?"
I said to the lady down the street
"My favourite colour is red," she said
"The colour of my favourite sweet."

"What's your favourite colour?"
I said to the girl at the school
"My favourite colour is blue," she said
"It makes me feel so cool."

"What's your favourite colour?"
I said to the boy down the row
"Every colour is my favourite," he said
"Especially those in a rainbow."

The Bird

I saw a bird in a nest
It started to cry
It said "I can't fly"

Try again I told it
I know you can
"I can't," it said

Give it one more go
Flap your wings
Look to the sky
And fly

Seasons

As new life starts
The life that grows
This new spring season
In time will show

That warm breeze
The heat of the sun
Those summer nights
Are so much fun

The falling leaves
That chill in the air
The autumn season
You'll always bear

That bitter wind
The frosty air
Those winter nights
Are always there

What to Eat?

Cornflakes are crunchy
Grapes can be sweet
Strawberries so tasty
Chips lovely to eat
Lemons are so bitter
Curry, nice and spicy
Burgers are so beefy
Sausages not too pricey
Spaghetti is so stringy
Custard nice and runny
Mousses are so textured
Syrup just like honey

So what to have to eat?

What a Sight

Look at the trees
How lovely they are
Viewing them from afar

Look at the sky
How pretty it is
It can't be missed

Look in the sea
How serene it lies
Under the pretty sky

The Storm

Rain, rain, rain
It's raining again
It's always the same

And with the rain comes
Thunder and lightning
In such a fierce storm

After the storm
You may see a rainbow
Such is the norm
After a storm

A Precious Thing

The most precious thing in life
Is money
Can't live without it

The most precious thing in life
Is water
Can't survive without it

The most precious thing in life
Is love
No happiness without it

The most precious thing in life
Is…
Life

Whales and Dolphins

What very
Huge and
Amazing animals
Living in the water
Enjoying every moment
Swimming in the sea

Dancing around
On the vast
Lovely ocean
Playing rather
Happily and
Irresistibly kind
Never tiring of
Swimming in the sea

Butterfly

I saw a butterfly
Flutter softly by
Gently beating its wings
As it floats in the sky

Bingo

Sitting in the grand hall
The caller calls them all
Eight, nineteen and sixty-three
We play along happily

On the gold book, page three
I'm waiting for 2 0 twenty
Here it is, now it's out
Time for a very loud shout

Bingo! Is the game I have won
A neat and very tidy sum
I have my money, what a sight
I'll go home smiling with delight.

The Little Crab

Sitting there
Alone and sad
Sarah's friend
The orange crab

In the post office
Left abandoned
Sarah saw it
And her heart saddened

Where did it come from?
Where had it been?
Sarah saved it
And put it on her screen.

Darts

I throw my darts
1, 2, 3
Hoping to score
Seventy-three
In the centre
Bullseye beckons
A score of fifty
Does so threaten
To finish the leg
Forty remains
A nice double twenty
We've won the game.

What Is a Baby?

What is a baby?
What do they do?
Listen to my tale
I'll tell you something new

They are new life
Which starts so small
After a few months
They'll start to crawl

Then as a toddler
Learning to walk
And not long after
Starting to talk

Sometimes born disabled
But with such big hearts
Need a little bit of help
To get that kick start

Going to school
And making friends
That's how this poem
Finally ends

But one last thought
To help all kids succeed
Give a donation
To Children In Need.

Sunrise

I sit at home
All alone
In the darkened room
In the midnight gloom

I sit and wait
For a sign
That the crescent moon
Will be going soon

And when it goes
The sky will glow
With orange and red
As the sun rises instead.

The Country Road

Driving down a country road
I looked out to the left

And what a sight did catch my eye
A car involved in a theft

Driving down a country road
I looked out to the right

And what a sight did catch my eye
It gave me such a fright

Driving down a country road
I looked out straight ahead

Do I see, what I think I see?
Is that me in bed?

Losing my focus I crashed the car
I fear my life. Am I dead?

Aargh! I wake up drenched in sweat
Not to worry though, I'm safe in bed.

More Similes

The wind whistles through the trees
   Like a wolf howling at its prey

The stars sparkle in the night sky
   Like the Sun shines on a sunny day

The leaves dance as they fall from the trees
   Like a child happily at play.

Weather Patterns

What strange weather we've had today
I want the sun and I wish it would stay

    For it started sunny
    Then it got cloudy
    It started to rain
    And I got drenched
    Then there was thunder
    Which followed the lightning
    Then snow, hail and sleet
    It was all rather frightening.

The Grand Day Out

It's a sunny day today
Where can I go?
I'll go to the circus
To see the big show

There are clowns on horseback
The ring master is there
On a trapeze is an acrobat
And a man is taming a bear

After the circus
I said I would meet
A few of my friends
Down on the beach

We'll swim in the ocean
Enjoy the warm sun
Play lots of beach sports
And have lots of fun.

My Puppy

I have a Dalmatian puppy at home
Spotty is his new name

He is so faithful and my best friend
I love him all the same

He comes to me when I call
When I call his name

With such a big smile on his face
He loves me all the same.

Bunch of Gibberish

A schizophrenic maniac
Was exceptionally gifted
With technological advancements

He was sophisticated
And was nervously anticipating
An occupational misunderstanding

Being unmistakably experimental
He underwent a transformation
From being supernaturally educational
To being functionally ambidextrous.

Retirement

As a young boy
At the age of eighteen
To be in the air force
Had been his dream

After many years' service
And how he'd liked to fly
He decided to touch down
To the sky he said goodbye

He came to the Post Office
And did that for his job
He retired on Saturday
Now we'll all sob.

At the Airport

Sat in the airport
After booking in
Ticket in hand
Moneys been changed
Plane is due anytime
I cannot wait
To get up in the air
Here I go
Plane is now boarding
I'm in the queue
Ticket has been checked
Not long now
I'm up in the air
And on my way.

Train Ride

I've never journeyed by train before
I wonder how it will be
And all the sights I'd see

Would it go on for hours and hours
Along the rails, the train will soar
Will I ever get bored?

I'd never travelled by train before
All the sights I saw
Looking out of the window
As the world flashed by
Under the clear blue sky.

Wind, Sun and Snow

I sit at home and listen
To the wind blowing outside
Gently moving leaves
As it blows through the trees

I sit and watch with awe
As the sun moves across the sky
Heating the ground
Never making a sound

I watch with fascination
As the snow starts to fall
Falling gently down
Laying on the ground.

My Story

I'm attempting to write a story
A science-fiction tale
I invite you all to read it
And hope I do not fail
It is about a girl
Who develops a disease
With once chance to save her
Her planet she must leave
A difficult process
She must undertake
Then finally, to her new life
From her sleep, she awakes
She has become an Elemental
And on this planet she stays
Until one day as danger looms
The planet Earth she saves.

I Can Dance

I'd like to learn a dance today
A hippy, jippy, jive
Since dancing makes me feel
So incredibly alive

What types of dance do I know?
The waltz and tango too
I'll also try the foxtrot
That is one I can do

So when I'm in a ballroom
And before me someone stands
To ask if I will dance
I'll gladly give my hand.

The Colours of Life

Red is for passion
A symbol of love

White stands for peace
Like the heavens above

Pink is embarrassment
A true friendship you hold

Blue denotes sadness
And can also mean cold

Black are the shadows
That hide in the night

Yellow could mean warmth
With the sun shining bright.

Final Words

These are my poems
Which don't always rhyme
I've tried so hard
To rhyme this time
They reminded me of times
When I was a kid
And all the good things
That I know I did
So when you're unhappy
And things are unkind
In my poems, I think you'll find
Your own peace of mind.

Vampires

Here are some poems you'll think are thrillers
Let's start with vampires, natural killers

Vampires have hearts which no longer beat
And bodies that cannot hold any heat

They are immortal and drink only blood
But with effort they can try to be good

So here is a warning for you to take heed
Vampires can move with such a high speed.

Me, A Vampire

Perhaps it's what I wanted
Maybe I wanted to be a vampire
So many things contributed to this

For example, I'd become immortal
Only one thing could kill me, fire
And I'd never fall ill or get weak

Then there's the never ending thirst
The thirst for human blood to drink
I'd be a killer, the best killer on the planet

And what about the family I'd leave behind
Could I really do that to them, they love me
Yes, I can because I want to live forever

That's how long I'd have, forever
Forever to watch them grow old and die
Whilst I never grew or changed a bit

I'd be dead to them, no heartbeat, no pulse
But I'd be alive a different way, walking but dead
And that's what I wanted
I had wanted to live forever
Well, now I can.

Slayer

As a slayer you'll find this easy

Fight the vampire and make him weaker

Hurt him with fire, burn him with a cross

A stake through the heart—that's his loss

My Last Night

Walking through the park last week
A strange man walked up to me
I thought to myself, *He's a freak*
I didn't realise what he was
Till he bent down to my neck
And started drinking my blood.

Vampire Tale

Vampires are evil
Vampires are cruel
They must drink blood
That is their fuel

Vampires are immortal
Vampires are cold
They're extremely fast
That's their story, told.

The Stranger

I watched him walk through the lonely night
He was pale and cold and looked quite a sight

He walked for ages then soon came to a stop
And decided that into a house he would pop

Then all of a sudden I heard a loud shout
And I went to see what it was about

That was a mistake but how could I see
The evil monster would then turn on me

From two large fangs was dripping blood
To run from him now would be no good

He came to me and held me so tight
Drank my blood, left me no strength to fight.

Vampire Mini Poems

There was once a vampire called Peter
And he is a bit of a cheater
He hunts once a week
And he's such a freak
Since he puts the spare blood in the freezer.

There was once a vampire called Bill
Who when hunting went in for the kill
He was very dozy
And for being so nosy
Got tied to a stake on a hill.

I once knew a vampire called Neil
Who drank human blood for his meals
It was a night in May
When I got in his way
And a painful death I did feel.

Witches

Here are some poems about witches
With magic, they turn rags to riches

Witches have warts which grow on their faces
Where they have been they leave no traces

In their cauldrons, vile potions they brew
If they go wrong, they start anew

They fly on broomsticks in the dead of night
Want to know about witches, here's an insight.

All About Witches

Cackle hee hee
Cackle haa haa
Witches are
Evil by far

In the cauldron
Stir the potion
This will be
An evil lotion

Broomsticks here
Broomsticks there
Flying Away
Through the air

Tale of the Witches

As I wandered down a dark, lonely street
Something extraordinary caught my eye
In the middle of this dark, lonely street
A very ancient house stood so high

You could tell it was old
From dust that had gathered on the sills
From the general state of the house
And the spiders sat in cobwebs on the walls

The dust on the windows was so immense
You could hardly see through the glass
And in the middle of the room, a cauldron
I watched for a while then saw a big flash

Then three old ladies came into view
Intoning spells and adding to the brew
These women are witches, that much I knew
And I didn't want to be part of their stew.

What Are Witches?

Witches are evil
Witches are hags
Witches are senseless
Witches are nags

Witches fly broomsticks
Witches cast spells
Witches brew potions
In darkness they dwell.

What a Sight!

Woke up early this morning
After hearing a funny noise
Imagine my surprise
When I saw
A witch

If it hadn't been for the crooked nose,
The black clothes and the broomstick

I would have had no idea.

My Friend, the Witch

In this world, there's one good witch
Her name is Sabrina

I know what you're thinking

How can I be sure she's good?
Easy

Five years ago she saved my life
We've been friends ever since

And to this day we've been together
The best of friends, always
Forever!

Witch Mini Poems

I knew a girl who was a witch
I found her frankly to be a bitch
Her name was Mary
And she was scary
Till they found her dead in a ditch.

There was once an old witch called Jess
Whose hair was always a mess
The people she hates
Because she has no mates
And she doesn't know how to dress.

I know a witch who is very young
After casting spells, she enjoys having fun
She's called Wendy
She is very trendy
And loves to go out in the sun.

Werewolves

Want to know about werewolves well here's a clue
Want knowledge and facts, I'll give you a few

A werewolf lives with secrets and lies
As a human they have the perfect disguise

When the full moon rises, they start to change
But for a werewolf this is not strange

After some years, they might learn a new trick
They could change anytime, if their anger can't stick.

The Transformation

There's this man, he's been acting very strange of late.
Every once in a while he disappears. I wonder why
as when he goes he's gone for three days at a time.

One day I decided to follow him to see where he goes.
He headed to the woods, then looked up at the sky.
As if anticipating something he waits. Then he goes in and I
creep a bit closer, its dusk now. I see
the moon starting to make an appearance. A full moon.
The man goes rigid, then falls heavily to his knees.

His nuzzle elongates, his face stretches to accommodate his
new features. His fingers grow longer and become claws.
His legs lengthen, now he has paws.
He is a werewolf.

Werewolf Haikus

I know a werewolf
He has a house down my street
And his name is Pete.

There is a wolfman
Who resides in the same town
As my friend from Down.

The sun is setting
The moon is about to rise
The howling begins.

After transforming
Now that he is a werewolf
He howls at the moon.

The Werewolf

Once every month
When the full moon rises
The man who is werewolf
Has a painful transformation
When the moon begins its rise
Till dawn the next day
In the werewolf form
He is forced to stay
For three nights a month
This form he must endure
For he is a werewolf
Of that I am sure.

What Is a Werewolf?

A werewolf is human most of the time
Except for three nights every month
The three nights of a full moon

The light of the moon touches their skin
And the painful transformation will begin
Each night of a full moon

Their bodies grow big and hairy
Definitely rather scary
On any night of a full moon

And they themselves grow quite wild
More uncontrollable than a small child
On the occasion of a full moon.

Full Moon

Looking out of the window on a cloudy night
Suddenly the full moon comes into my sight
Then I hear it, the howling of wolves
Their transformation begun and I'm no fool
Lock doors, lock windows and stay in my room
Till dawn approaches and thus sets the full moon.

The Wolf

If you're out in the woods
And you meet a wolf

Be careful

He might be a werewolf

If you're out all alone
And he comes into view

Be careful
Don't let him bite you!

Werewolf Mini Poems

Here is a werewolf called Bruce
With the townsfolk, he set up a truce
He killed for meals
Thus broke his deal
And ended up hung in a noose.

I know a werewolf called Charlie
Who survives on wheat and barley
I think you will find
That he's lost his mind
Because he thinks he's Bob Marley.

There was once a werewolf called Ben
Who lived in a house over the glen
He got quite shirty
Since he was thirty
And had been bitten when he was ten.

Ghosts

Here are some poems you might understand
Ever felt something cold touch your hand?

Realise that there's no one in the room
And you see a face hanging in the gloom

That is impossible, they're not really there
You know it's a ghost, which gives you a scare

I hope you read on and try to be brave
You should enjoy them if its ghosts you crave.

Anyone There?

Knock knock!

Who's there?

Knock knock!

I said who's there?

Knock knock!

Who is it?

Knock knock!

You're scaring me!

Walking to the door I see that nobody is there.

A Ghost's Song

As a ghost he'll live on through this life

He had a daughter and he had a wife

He'd seen the wars and so much strife

It was too much so he took a knife

Now he's stuck he can't move on

A century later his family's gone

Reasons to stay here, he has none

But still he's here to sing this song.

Poltergeist

Poltergeists are noisy ghosts
They'll move your possessions
To try to confuse you

Sometimes they'll smash things
Or make objects fly
Want to see one you just try

Because poltergeists like to hide.

Haunted House

I went to a theme park
Just last week
To the haunted house
To take a peek
Went inside
And walked around
Suddenly I heard a sound
I spun around and there I saw
A person hovering
Above the floor
That was a ghost
It had to be

Then it vanished.

What Does a Ghost Look Like?

Are they see-through?
Are they opaque?
Do they sleep at night?
Or lie awake?

Are they happy?
Or are they sad?
Are they friendly?
Or downright bad?

I don't know
I haven't seen one.

The Plight

Look at him
All pearly white
What a state
What a plight

A horrid death
He just went through
What was coming
He'd had no clue

He fell off a cliff
Right into the ocean
As if it were
In slow motion

So here he is
Stuck in this state
With all eternity
Now to wait.

The Ghost

I look in a mirror
There's a man behind me
I turn around

And he's gone
Was he a ghost?

Noises in an Empty House

Walked into a deserted house
Heard a noise behind the door
Nothing there

Ascended the creaky stairs
A noise over there
Nothing there

Went across the landing
Heard a noise in the bedroom
Looked in the room
A chill swept past me
I turned around
Something's there

A figure
Pearly white
A ghost.

Ghost Mini Poems

Susan became a ghost one night in May
She had decided to go out for the day
She slipped and fell
Became quite unwell
And that was the night she passed away.

Brian was a ghost who liked fast cars
He died one night whilst watching the stars
A ghost he became
But he wasn't the same
He decided instead to haunt local bars.

There was once a ghost named Jade
Who lived for the future she had made
They thought it funny
To kill her for money
Now she haunts them from the shade.

Dragons

Dragons are the subject of this next lot
Let's look at the abilities that they've got

Starting with the fire they breathe through their lips
And when it comes to flying they'll give you some tips

Dragons can be good, dragons can be bad
Watching them hurt people makes me so mad

Of the good dragons, there are quite a few
If you're good to them, they'll be good to you.

To Know a Dragon

I've seen lots of dragons in my time
Many different colours too
I know dragons that are white,
Red, green and blue
I even know a purple one
You should see these magnificent beasts
They stand so proud and tall
Of all the beings from the supernatural world
Dragons are my favourites of them all.

What Are Dragons Like?

There are many dragons in this world
And a lot of them are bad
But look around and you might find
A dragon that is good

Some breathe fire
Some breathe ice
Some are naughty
Some are nice
Some are fat
Some are small
Some are thin
And some are tall

If you meet a dragon
Look at him and see
How he'll react to you
And if he'll leave you be.

Many Dragons

Dancing rays of light
Reflect off their hinds
And all around them
Glistens in the midday sun
Overlooking the meadow
Near to the other dragons.

Take Flight

Soaring along in the sky
Underneath me, a dragon
With widespread wings
And a sturdy back
He soars along happily
Flapping his wings
Up and down they go
And the cool breeze
Blows past my face
As we fly through the sky.

A Proud Dragon

The sun pasted beams of glittering light
On a magnificent sight
The dragon

Sat proudly in his meadow
Wings spread out
Reflecting the rays of the sun
In a tremendous rainbow of colour
How proud he must be
The dragon

With his scaly hind
Strong legs and talons
And his ability to breathe fire
He must be so proud

The dragon.

What Can a Dragon Do?

Dragons are magical flying beasts
Flying high, accomplishing great feats

Their talons are sharp and so very long
Their bodies are big and so very strong

From their mouths, they breathe fire or ice
Anger a dragon and you'll pay a high price.

Dragon Mini Poems

There was once a dragon called Igor
High in the sky he liked to soar
They watched and admired
As he sat and breathed fire
And this gave him something to live for.

I knew a dragon whose name was Rose
She was delighted in the life she had chose
Her colour was red
She breathed ice instead
For when she breathed fire, she burned her toes.

I once knew a dragon called Pete
A blue dragon you'd like to meet
He breathed fire and ice
Enjoyed eating rice
And lived at the end of my street.

Mythical Beings

These are poems about other mythical beings
About fairies and angels which both have wings

There's unicorns, demons and leprechauns too
And Santa who'll come down the chimney for you

Also Hades and centaurs and a thought I will lend
Have you ever had an imaginary friend?

Mermaids, elves and nymphs are last on the list
To give these poems such a good twist.

Fairies

Enter a garden
What do you see?
I see a fairy
Flying near a tree

Guarding nature
Helping it grow
Look at it fly
With grace and flow

There are fairies for flowers
And fairies for trees
Fairies for rivers
And fairies for seas

They're always there
Very rarely seen
Fairies guard nature
And help keep it green.

The Fairy

Sat in my garden
What do I see
A fairy hiding in a tree
And when I look closer
What do I see
That this fairy is free
Free to go anywhere
Be what she wants to be
A fairy hiding in a tree.

The Elegance of Unicorns

Spreading their magic across the lands
The legendary unicorn
So picturesque
And purely white
What a sight to see
With magic in their horn
And elegance in their stride
What a magnificent creature
That in this world does feature.

Unicorns

Unicorns are magical, the essence of nature
They are pure of heart and pure of soul
Looking like horses but always so white
Have a horn protruding from their heads
If you see one be grateful and keep this in mind
Unicorns by nature are always very kind.

Demons

Red
Green
Black
White
Blue
Yellow
Dark
Light

These are some of the colours
That a demon might be
They are pure evil
And that you will see.

What Is a Demon?

Demons are the evils that roam the lands
They travel in packs and hunt with their hands
They come in many different shapes
To see them makes you want to gape
You'd be in danger, you'd better run
Since most of the demons, hate the sun.

Demons, What Are They Like?

Demons come in many shapes
And many different sizes

Knowing some basic facts
Will make you all the wiser

Some of them are small and fat
And some of them are lean

Most of them are quite tall
But mainly are unclean

They have different features
Like long fingers and toes

Some of them have horns
Or a very big nose

Some can move extremely fast
Whilst some of them are slow

If you see one approaching you
A wise move would be to go.

The Mermaid

In the deep blue water
Out in the ocean
Keep eyes wide open
There is motion
A beautiful woman
Could it really be
A mermaid is swimming
Heading towards me.

Mermaids

Their faces are beautiful
They move so serene
Their bodies so streamline
Their tails are so green

Half human, half fish
They live in the sea
Singing their songs
And living so free

These are the mermaids
They swim oh so swift
Be good to them all
They may give you a gift.

Nymphs

Go into the forest and you might find
A forest nymph amongst the trees
Venture into the ocean and you might see
A sea nymph amongst the waves

These are the guardians of nature
They help trees and flowers grow
Watch them as they do their work
You'll see them on the go.

Elf

An elf lives in an elven house
Down an elven street
In an elven town
Near an elven city
And an elven wood
In an elven country
That's all good

An elfish person
Is tall and thin
With pointy ears
And perfect skin
They live in groups
Of elfish kin
That's how the life of an elf
Would begin.

Imaginary Friend (Part 1)

I'd like you to meet someone
Her name is Belle
We do everything together

We share the same toys
Sleep in the same bed
Tell stories to each other
Cuddle up to dear old ted

But as I grow older
And now I am four
My imaginary friend
Isn't there anymore

Bye bye Belle.

Imaginary Friend (Part 2)

I'm twenty-four now
How time has flown
For now, I'm an adult
I am fully grown

I now have a daughter
Megan she is called
She has no friends
No one at all

So I told her a story
A story about Belle
My imaginary friend
A good story to tell

Now Megan has a friend
And Belle is always there
To keep my Megan company
That's one good friend we share.

Leprechaun

Gold, gold lots of gold
A leprechaun has a pot of gold
Over the rainbow
Right at the end
Leprechauns are always
The best of friends.

Lost

Standing easily upon his four legs
I see in the distance a centaur

Bottom half horse
Top half man
I quickly scan
He's all alone

Do I move closer?
Or will I scare him?
And if he hears me
What do I do?
Should I run?
Or should I stay?
I'll leave him alone
He'll go on his way
He moves closer
I stand quite still
He touches my arm
And gives me a chill
"Hello," he says
"Are you lost?"

Hades

I had a nightmare last night
There was a terrible fight
Then everything went white

And somebody spoke
That's when I woke
I saw it was a bloke

"I'm Charon," he said
"Your ferryman," he said
He looked at me and said, "You're dead,"

"Now get on the boat,
We Must cross this moat,"
So smoothly we did float

"In Hades you must stay
Forever and a day,"
I heard him say
When moments later in bed I lay.

Father Christmas

Big red suit
Big black boots
He comes down the chimney
With a sack full of loot

Gifts for girls
Gifts for boys
They will be happy
Playing with their toys.

Christmas Time

What a perfect time of year—Christmas
All the good girls and boys
Get lots of toys

Lots of fun under the Christmas tree
Happy times for the family

What a perfect time of year
Join in all the festivities
And Christmas activities
Delivered by Father Christmas.

Be Good at Christmas

Once a year Father Christmas comes to call
To bring presents to one and all
To girls and boys who've been good this year
And help to spread some festive cheer
So be good to all, the young and the old
That is the message, now you've been told.

Angels

The wings of an angel
So heavenly white
They come from above
Where all is so bright

A halo of gold
Hangs over their head
Their footprints leave beauty
Wherever they've tread.

What Is an Angel?

Angelic features
Angelic faces
They're always going places

Guiding people
Helping people
Doing what they can

Dressed in white
With white wings
How angelic they sing

Their voices soft
And souls so pure
So heavenly they are for sure.

Supernatural

Vampires are extremely fast
Witches are a thing of the past
Werewolves change on a full moon
Ghosts are dead, they'll move on soon
Dragons can fly and breathe fire
From the supernatural most things transpire.

How to Recognise a Supernatural Being?

When you're all alone
You need to know
How to spot them
And how does it show?

A vampire you will find
Is cold and has fangs

A werewolf you will see
During a full moon becomes furry

A ghost you will know
For scares, he's a pro

A witch you'll discover
Remains part of her coven.

A World of Fantasy

And all around us is magic
You will see that life is tragic
Without the magic

Nymphs look after the oceans
Whilst fairies look after the flowers
Elves take care of the forests
It requires lots of powers

Using this good magic.

Supernatural Beings

We live in a world of the supernatural
All around us there are vampires, werewolves and witches
Most of them are vicious
Vampires are suspicious
Werewolves are malicious
Witches superstitious
This is the world of the supernatural.

Miscellaneous Mini Poems 1

I know a fairy called Laura
All of the fairies adore her
She cares for flowers
With magical powers
So the fairies nicknamed her Flora.

There was once an elf named Den
He lived with his friends in the glen
He has a blast
'cause he runs so fast
That when racing he beats all the men.

There was once a young nymph called Nell
She has such a good story to tell
She lives in a fountain
Next to a mountain
Which is mistaken for a wishing well.

Miscellaneous Mini Poems 2

I know Santa, his name is Saint Nick
He eats mince pies and makes himself sick
Once every year
He brings festive cheer
And I promise this isn't a trick.

My friend Jasmine is a unicorn
On her forehead is a spiralling horn
She is pure white
Oh what a sight
And from pure magic she is born.

There was once a demon called Fred
Who has two horns on his head
He's very mean
And coloured green
Or you'd think he was the devil instead.